PK Reader • SOCIAL STUDIES

Reading Level: **1–2** Interest Level: **1–3**

A Trip to the Farm

When you think of a farm, you may picture chickens and pigs, or corn and wheat. But some farms have other kinds of plants and animals. Some farms, called orchards, have fruit trees. People at horse farms raise horses! In this set, readers will explore four kinds of farms to see what it's like to work on one and what those farms produce. Vibrant photographs of crops, animals, and farmers are paired with manageable text to ensure a comprehensive learning experience.

- The text was carefully crafted to help young readers comprehend potentially difficult topics and terms
- The role of community helpers is an essential component of early elementary social studies instruction
- Life cycles and agriculture are essential components of the early elementary science curriculum

NEW FALL 2022!

School & Library Price reflects 25% off the List Price

Library-bound Book		S&L **$18.45**
eBook		S&L **$18.45**
4-Book Print Set		S&L **$73.80** 978-1-5383-8736-8

TITLE	DEWEY	GRL	ATOS	©
① **Crop Farms** Ursula Pang • 978-1-7253-3951-4 eBook: 978-1-7253-3952-1	RR13414	H	① PENDING	©2023
② **Dairy Farms** Ursula Pang • 978-1-7253-3947-7 eBook: 978-1-7253-3948-4	RR13415	H	② PENDING	©2023
③ **Horse Farms** Ursula Pang • 978-1-7253-3943-9 eBook: 978-1-7253-3944-6	RR13416	H	③ PENDING	©2023
④ **Orchards** Ursula Pang • 978-1-7253-3939-2 eBook: 978-1-7253-3940-8	RR13417	H	④ PENDING	©2023

Reading Level: **1–2**   Interest Level: **1–3**

8 ½" x 8 ½" • Library Binding • 24 pp. • Full-Color Photographs • Further Information Section • Glossary • Index

① RR13414   ② RR13415

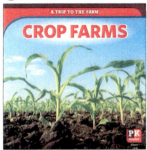 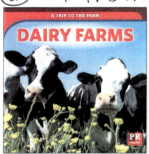

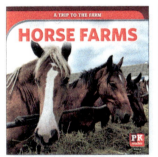 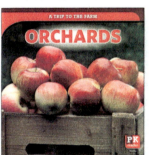

③ RR13416   ④ RR13417

Actual Type Size

A TRIP TO THE FARM

CROP FARMS

URSULA PANG

New York

Published in 2023 by The Rosen Publishing Group, Inc.
29 East 21st Street, New York, NY 10010

Copyright © 2023 by The Rosen Publishing Group, Inc.

All rights reserved. No part of this book may be reproduced in any form without permission in writing from the publisher, except by a reviewer.

First Edition

Editor: Greg Roza
Designer: Leslie Taylor

Photo Credits: Cover Lamyai/Shutterstock.com; series artwork (background) OHishiapply/Shutterstock.com; p. 5 Jack Frog/Shutterstock.com; p. 7 DedovStock/Shutterstock.com; p. 9 dugdax/Shutterstock.com; p. 11 Luis Echeverri Urrea/Shutterstock.com; p. 13 (jute) Md. Murad Hossain/Shutterstock.com; p. 13 (cotton) muratart/Shutterstock.com; p. 13 (flax) Sergey Cherviakov/Shutterstock.com; p. 15 duchic/Shutterstock.com; p. 17 BearFotos/Shutterstock.com; p. 19 (tractors) Krizek Vaclav/Shutterstock.com; p. 19 (inset) Artie Medvedev/Shutterstock.com p. 21 Rawpixel.com/Shutterstock.com.

Cataloging-in-Publication Data

Names: Pang, Ursula.
Title: Crop farms / Ursula Pang.
Description: New York : Powerkids Press, 2023. | Series: A trip to the farm | Includes glossary and index.
Identifiers: ISBN 9781725339491 (pbk.) | ISBN 9781725339514 (library bound) | ISBN 9781725339507 (6pack) | ISBN 9781725339521 (ebook)
Subjects: LCSH: Food crops–Juvenile literature. | Plants–Juvenile literature. | Farms–Juvenile literature.
Classification: LCC SB175.P364 2023 | DDC 630–dc23

Manufactured in the United States of America

Some of the images in this book illustrate individuals who are models. The depictions do not imply actual situations or events.

CPSIA Compliance Information: Batch #CSPK23. For Further Information contact Rosen Publishing, New York, New York at 1-800-237-9932.

CONTENTS

On the Farm 4
Yummy Crops 6
Animal Feed 8
Oilseed Crops 10
Textiles 12
Just for Show 14
Farm Workers 16
Farm Technology 18
At the Market 20
Glossary 22
For Further Information 23
Index 24

On the Farm

Crops are plants that are grown on farms. There are many different kinds of crops! We use these plants for many uses. We eat a lot of crops. Some crops are used to make **textiles**. Others are used to feed animals.

Yummy Crops

Food farms grow food for everyone! Crop farms grow fruits, vegetables, seeds, and nuts. Some grow grains, such as wheat, corn, and rice. Some grow plants used for seasoning foods, such as cinnamon and black pepper.

Animal Feed

Some farms grow grasses and grains that we give to animals. Most of these crops are grown to feed livestock. Livestock are animals such as cows, pigs, and sheep. Crops used to feed animals include clover and barley. Some livestock eat grass in a field.

barley field

Oilseed Crops

Some crop farms grow plants for the oil in their seeds. Oils are used in cooking. Oilseed plants include sunflowers, peanuts, and coconut trees. About 90 percent of oilseed crops in the United States are soybean crops.

Textiles

Some crops are grown for their tough **fibers**. These include cotton, jute, and flax. They are used to make textiles. Some of the clothes we wear are made out of textiles. These fibers are also used to make bedding, curtains, rope, and much more.

Just for Show

Some crops are used for **decoration**. These kinds of plants include house plants, flowers, trees, and bushes. People often buy these plants at businesses called **nurseries**. Many nurseries grow their own crops. Some are grown inside a greenhouse!

Farm Workers

The workers on crop farms have many jobs. They plant seeds and **saplings** and care for the growing crops. Workers gather crops several times a year. Other crops, such as trees, may need more time to grow.

Farm Technology

People have been growing crops for thousands of years. Farmers have long used hand tools. Today, new **technology** makes crop farming easier. Farmers use tractors to do much of the work. There are machines to plant seeds and machines to gather crops.

At the Market

Without crop farms, we wouldn't have our favorite foods. The plants grown on crop farms are sold to people and businesses. You can find them at the supermarket! Some farmers sell their own crops. You may like to visit a farmers market.

GLOSSARY

decoration: Something that adds beauty to a space or an object.

fiber: Tough plant material that is used to make cloth.

nursery: A place where plants and trees are grown and sold.

sapling: A young tree.

technology: A method that uses science to solve problems and the tools used to solve those problems.

textile: A woven or knit cloth.

FOR FURTHER INFORMATION

WEBSITES

Crops
www.nationalgeographic.org/encyclopedia/crop/
Visit this website to learn much more about crop farming all over the world.

What Is a Farm?
www.twinkl.com/teaching-wiki/farm
This website has information on different kinds of farms.

BOOKS

Gardeski, Christina Mia. *A Year on the Farm.* North Mankato, MN: Pebble, 2020.

Sutton, Sally. *Tractor.* Somerville, MA: Candlewick, 2022.

Publisher's note to parents and teachers: Our editors have reviewed the websites listed here to make sure they're suitable for students. However, websites may change frequently. Please note that students should always be supervised when they access the internet.

INDEX

A
animals, 4, 8

D
decoration, 14

F
farmers market, 20
fibers, 12
food farms, 6

G
gather crops, 16, 18
greenhouse, 14
grains, 6, 8

H
hand tools, 18

L
livestock, 8

N
nurseries, 14

O
oilseed crops, 10

S
seasoning, 6
seeds, 10, 16, 18
soybean crops, 10
supermarket, 20

T
technology, 18
textiles, 4, 12
tractors, 18

W
workers, 16